# Get Me Out of Here!

Valerie Wilding
Illustrated by Sarah Warburton

# Chapters

# Chapter 1 *Stop Fussing!*

Dear Miss Pumpkin,

Once upon a time, you helped a young girl called Cinderella. She was sad and lonely, but now she is a happy princess.

Now I need the help of a fairy godmother. I'm tired of living in this old palace. I'm the only child here and there is nothing for me to do! The palace is full of old servants who never stop fussing over me. My parents fuss over me too!

I want to be more like other boys and have lots of friends around me. I need your help to get me out of here!

Prince Percy

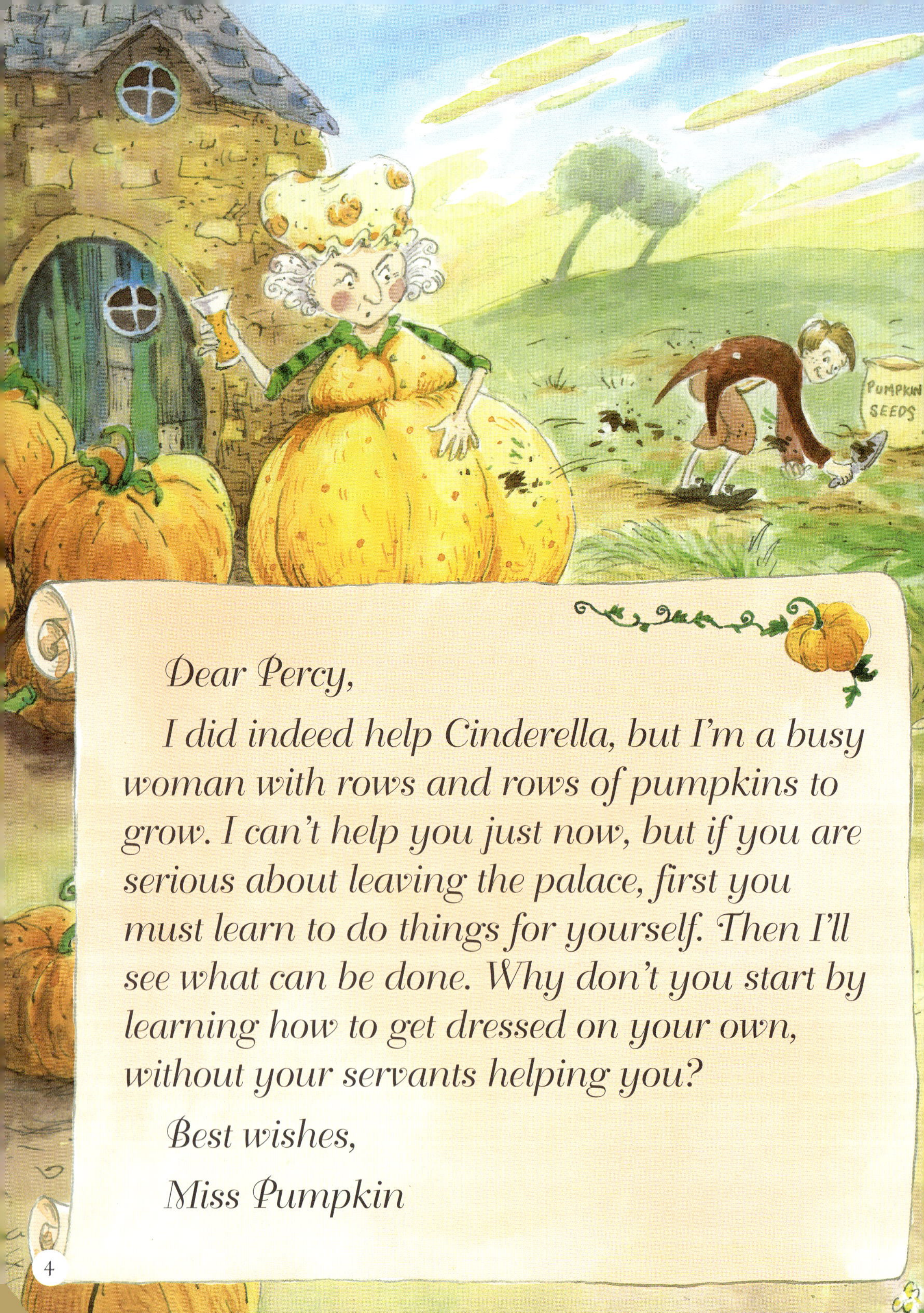


*Dear Percy,*

*I did indeed help Cinderella, but I'm a busy woman with rows and rows of pumpkins to grow. I can't help you just now, but if you are serious about leaving the palace, first you must learn to do things for yourself. Then I'll see what can be done. Why don't you start by learning how to get dressed on your own, without your servants helping you?*

*Best wishes,*

*Miss Pumpkin*

Dear Miss Pumpkin,

I just had to write to tell you that I can look after myself now. This morning I washed myself and dressed myself. I even combed my hair and made my own bed! Surely I'm ready to leave the palace now?

Percy

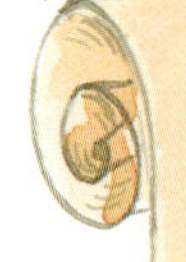

*Dear Percy,*

*Well that's a start I suppose! But if you really want to leave the palace and stand on your own two feet, you must learn how to work for a living. Look at the people who work in the palace. Watch what they do and learn from them.*

*Regards,*

*Miss Pumpkin*

Dear Miss Pumpkin,

You will be very proud of me. I've learned to work! Last night, I served Mother her dinner and today, when I saw that my book had fallen, I picked it up all by myself. Then, when Father asked the maid to bring him a pen, I said I would do it.

Father thought it was kind of me to bring him his pen but I soon explained that it was not kindness, it was work.

I'm sure that I can hold my own in the big, wide world. Are you ready to get me out of here yet?

Percy

# Chapter 2 *Housework Too!*

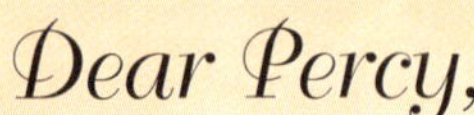

*Dear Percy,*

*Well, it seems that you are trying hard, but there is much more to learn! To hold your own in the big, wide world, you must do more than pick up a fallen book or take your father a pen. You must learn how to do real work. Start with some housework, but be careful with the windows!*

*Miss Pumpkin*

Dear Miss Pumpkin,

Help! I don't understand. What is housework? Did Cinderella do housework?

Percy

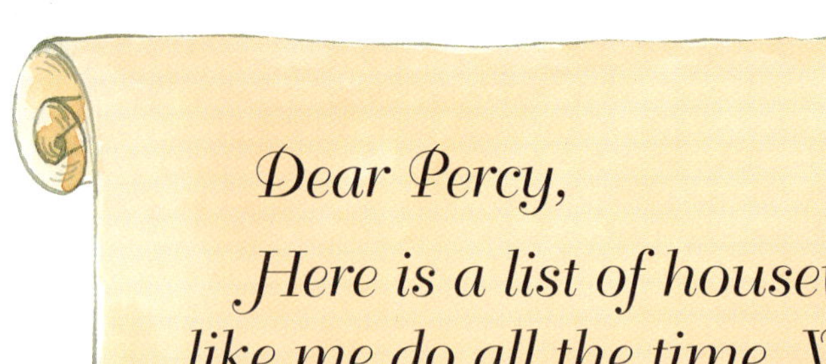

Dear Percy,

Here is a list of housework that people like me do all the time. You must learn to do them too.

- Washing and ironing
- Cleaning
- Cooking
- Shopping

Give housework a try!

Good luck!

Miss Pumpkin

Dear Miss Pumpkin,

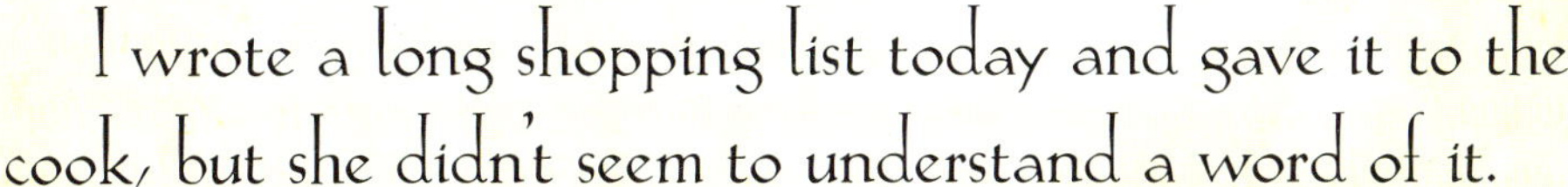

I wrote a long shopping list today and gave it to the cook, but she didn't seem to understand a word of it.

Next, I turned my hand to cooking. I made two apple pies, seven cakes and eight muffins. One of the maids was so impressed, she just stopped and stared at me.

I was enjoying myself so much I then washed the windows and cleaned the floors. I don't need servants any more. I have mastered housework just like you wanted me to.

Please write to me straight away. I must know when you're going to get me out of here!

Percy

Dear Percy,

Your cooking sounds impressive, but what about doing the washing and the ironing for yourself too? There is much more housework for you to learn before you can leave the palace.

All the best,

Miss Pumpkin

Dear Miss Pumpkin,

MORE housework? All right. Tomorrow I'll wash and iron all the clothes in the palace myself. But please be ready to get me out of here!

Percy

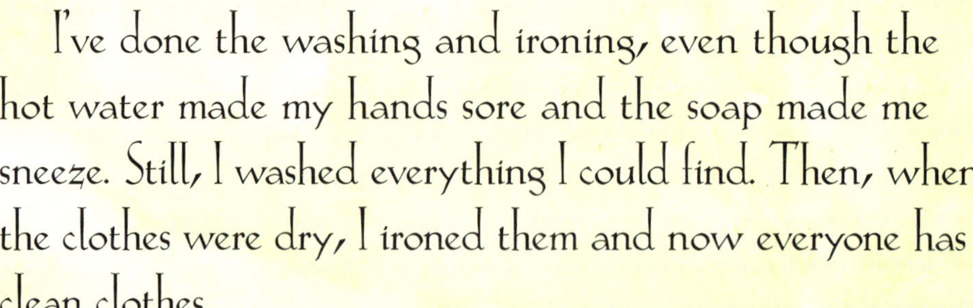

Dear Miss Pumpkin,

I've done the washing and ironing, even though the hot water made my hands sore and the soap made me sneeze. Still, I washed everything I could find. Then, when the clothes were dry, I ironed them and now everyone has clean clothes.

I've done it all myself. Surely there's nothing left to learn. Now will you GET ME OUT OF HERE?

Percy

# Chapter 3 The Great Outdoors

*Dear Percy,*

*Yes, you have learned about the housework in the palace. But hold on! What about work outside the palace? There are dogs, horses and gardens, and they all need looking after. You still have a lot to learn, my dear. You are not ready to leave the palace yet! Now I must go and work hard in my own garden.*

*Regards,*

*Miss Pumpkin*

Dear Miss Pumpkin,

I've done lots of work outside today. I fed the horses, washed the dogs and cut the grass in the garden. But the servants still want to do the work too. I don't know why!

I can't hold on any longer. Please come along to the palace and GET ME OUT OF HERE!

Percy

*Dear Percy,*

*I'm not coming to get you until you can hold your own in the big, wide world. Your coachman drives you everywhere and you would get lost outside the palace grounds. There are many more things to learn – trust me. I shall write a list for you if I ever get a moment.*

*Best wishes,*

*Miss Pumpkin*

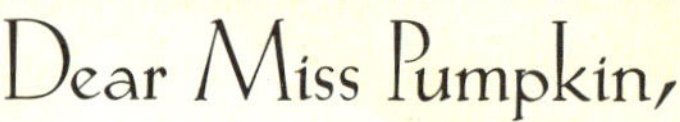

Dear Miss Pumpkin,

I've had enough! I've done everything you said but you still haven't come to GET ME OUT OF HERE! I can't stay in this old palace any more. I'm packing my bags. Be at the palace gate tomorrow morning, or I will come to your cottage. I will stay with you until I can survive on my own in the big, wide world.

Percy

Special Message!

Percy,

You don't need to come to my cottage as I am sending my servant, Sam, to the palace to help you learn how to do more things. With Sam's help, you will be able to leave the palace and hold your own in the big, wide world.

All the best,

Miss Pumpkin

# Chapter 4 *Teaching Percy*

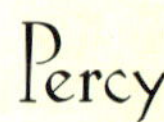

Dear Miss Pumpkin,

Sorry I haven't written for so long, but I have been very busy. Sam is teaching me how to do even more things around the palace and I am doing very well.

The servants are still fussing over me, though, so Sam will have to stay here awhile to teach me even more. I hope this is OK. Sam and I get along well and it's nice to be with someone my age. Things aren't so bad at the palace now.

Percy

Dear Miss Pumpkin,

I miss living in your cottage with you. Prince Percy works hard, but he gets things wrong all the time! I could be teaching him how to work forever!

Please say I can come back to your cottage now!

Best wishes,

Sam

Dear Percy,

Have fun with Sam, but don't wear him out! I know how hard all that work is, but keep at it! Remember practice makes perfect!

Kind regards,

Miss Pumpkin

Dear Sam,

Don't let Percy wear you out. I know Percy needs to learn how to work, but he needs a friend even more. I do hope you'll become friends. Please don't worry about staying at the palace. I am quite happy on my own.

All the best,

Miss Pumpkin

Dear Miss Pumpkin,
Prince Percy still can't do housework properly. He's really happy all the time but I can't take it any longer.
Now, I need your help. Please say you will GET ME OUT OF HERE!
Sam
Gone Away!